To those who know
what happens in a cocoon

SACRED PROTEST

POEMS BY
ANTONNETTE ASARE

part one

Joyful Rebellion

There's joy
In this rebellion
Boot tracks
On newborn snow
Storm clouds
Of crowds gather
Together shouting
"No!"

There are dreams
On the horizon
Imaginations grow
Raw
Earthy
Witchy
Goodness
May it spread
May it flow

Finding Purpose

Some work is sacred
Journey to the
Deep and cavernous
Take trepid footsteps
Interlock arms

The blinding darkness
Reveals the light
In hindsight
Until then
Inch along
Believe the next step
To be
The right one

Sacred work is
That which you
Need to do
Guided by
Moral compass or
Artful play
An aching hunger
That disturbs sleep
A pain that won't go away
Until
Your body moves
Stretches into space
While a filling breath
Gives deep joy

Find this work
You'll know it
It seems like heaven
Bent itself to guide
You

Surreptitious

Words have shifted
East
Lit with new meanings
Words have shifted
West
Set
Unspoken

So I speak the moon
Mercy
Memory
Story
Love
Before the eclipse

The First Raindrop

I discover
I am a raindrop
Formed in the gray
Stratus of tyranny
I don't understand
Why
Those sauntering
On the ground
Can not see
The lack of sunshine or
Notice the wind
Seeking cracks in
Places long in disrepair

I embrace
My purpose
Fall from the sky
Unafraid of vengeful winds
One joyous glide
A fling with form
I land
Upon your face with
Intimate softness
You look up to
Realize
It is
Raining

Banned/Banished

You
Purged the books
Snuffed the last crinkled
Gasps
Of dusty untouched pages
Painted white the shelves
The walls, the chairs
Sealed the blinds
Stacked the shelves with myths
Americana

They WILL read your name in
The future
You
Are the lesson

Interior Decorating

When beds are made cruelly
One lies awake and aches
Pale linen sheets are stale
In spring when the world outside
Is rich with rhymes and rainbows

A valence allows a strip of light
Revealing empty spaces where
A handcrafted mahogany could
Add a touch of grace
The bedroom has ruthless purpose
It's where a body sleeps

When its time to sell
Sly descriptions
And select pictures
Fill the open house
Buyers flee
The bedroom
Haunted and hollow

Youthful Disobedience

Have you ever seen
A successful movement
Without the energy and
Disobedience of youth?

Defying and disrupting
The planned rhythms
Of every day
Meant to extract and contain
Order your steps
With the ideas of the 'leaders'

What is it
That you **must** do today
What would
Happen if you didn't?
Live a day
In refusal
With a thousand others
One hundred thousand others

These actions have names
Boycott
Strike
Disobedience
In the language of the 'leaders'
Insubordinate
Troublemaker
Terrorist

Beekeeper

as we pollinate our places
in the morning flow
ideas spread faster than
the light we know
we give our best
for a distant queen
who rates our efforts
and is sometimes mean
we toil, rain or shine
happy, sad, or feeling fine
but the beekeeper
we worship
for only he knows
the markets and shops
where honey goes

part two

Coming Home From a Night Shift

A rabbit darts
Into shadows
Fur brown as dormant grass
A brief speck
In gazing headlights
During the predawn chill

The houses
Still sleeping
Some waking
Perhaps
The sky a surreal painting
Dimming light bulbs
Waking sun

A lonely engine
Whirs to a stop at
A two-car garage
Feet
Lug up steps
Body
Collapses in bed
The world says
Good morning

What Happens When You're Wounded

Lions roar
      My ears perk
Snap of crunchy grass
Thud of stomping feet
      Upon steps
I sprint
When I'm caught
I feel
      Sting of leather
      Upon my backside
      Claws upon skin
Never going for the kill
Just wound and warn and discipline
Run faster
Next time
Or wait
Until
I'm not a cub
When my teeth
And roar are
      Just as fierce
But then
I have become
      A hunter

Words From a Teenage Journal

Falling
Needing a hand
To catch my lonely soul
Powerful heaven saving me
Rising

Laughter
Heavenly sound
Curing human sadness
Requisite for facing hardships
Sobbing

When You Want to Perish

Bury me
Six feet above
The sun
In a space
No one can find
Where hope
Cannot tempt me
With fragrant promises
Where my tears
Can mist onto
Lonely streets
Where stray cats
Roam
Darting
Playfully
In storm drains
In early morning

Bury me deep
On the horizon
In the hues
Of sky
Where my struggles
Fade behind
Twilight palettes
Where the melodies of spring
Dowse my pleas

I never
Have to face
The night
Again

Keepin' On

If I wake up
I'll see the sun
Strength is worn
Not yet done
I'm steeled
Yet groovin'
Movin' on
Sealed
Till disprov'n
Keepin' on

If I mess up
Let it be
Quitters quit
Not me!
I'm healed and
Steppin'
Walkin' on
Life I'm reppin'
Keepin' on

Texas Pirates

He stutters
But
Words march
From his mouth like
A nimble crew
"Put your hands on the wheel!"
My hands shakily search
Clutch the helm of this captured ship
I am ordered to step upon the plank
Another pirate sails up
Eyes wander through my ship
Lacking gold doubloons
My ship is free to sail
But
This captain
Forever sunken

Discharge Instructions

I was cut
From the womb
Ahead of schedule
Wrapped in the umbilical cord
They said
Perhaps I knew something
Maybe
The unborn see
The song of their lives
With the clarity of night sky
Without light pollution

A white doctor
Removed me
From my intended resting place
Brought forth a baby
Brown as toast
Then released me
To the world

There should have been instructions
Seek medical attention if you notice:
Hatred because of the color of your skin
Rigid expectations of masculinity
Domestic violence
A society obsessed with thinness
Violence, war, genocide, and poverty
An irrational hatred of women

Now therapy

Sweet Potato Pie for the Soul

I wish I could make Grandmother's
Sweet potato pie
The way she would
Dot the kitchen counter with flour
Mold a sticky ball of dough
With limber fingers
Sweet orange filling cooled
Yielding a perfect slice
Not too soft
Not too firm

I never learned her secrets
But I'll never forget
Warm cinnamon and nutmeg
Lingering on my tongue

I make my own pies
Close, but
Not the same
For those of a different race
A different time
A different place
I understand
What she passed on
To me

part three

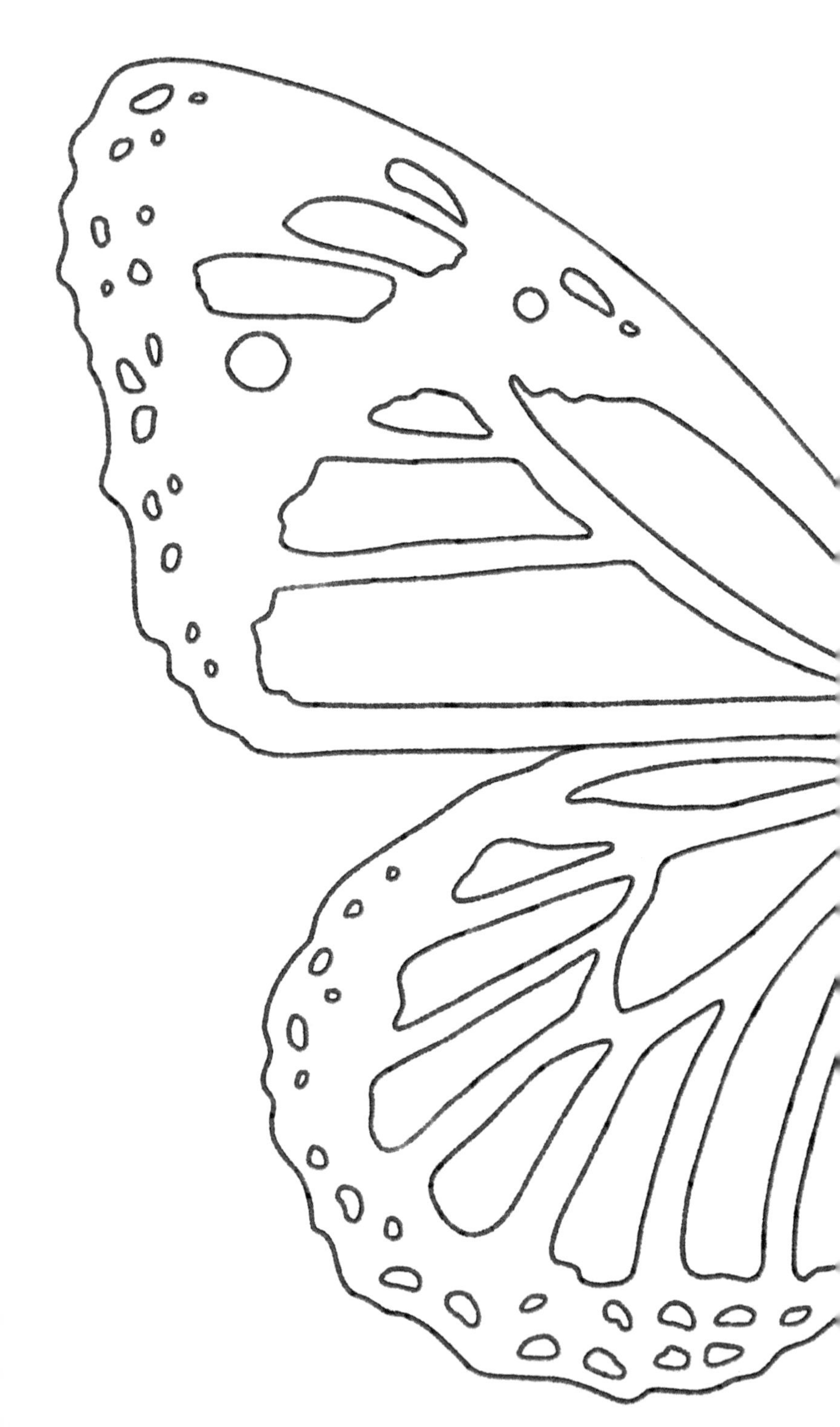

That Thing in the Sky

If I were born with wings
Surgeons would
Remove them
Tell my parents I am disordered
How difficult my life will be

As I grow up
I would be
Laughed at
Ostracized
Encouraged to hide

In my teens
I would secretly practice
Gliding through the night sky
Dancing in the moonlight
Making shapes with the stars

Now
The world falls apart
Fires, floods, winds
Laws being broken
Ethics turned clay
I would take to the sky
With outstretched arms
For the least of these

Space Traveler

When did I cross the chasm
Of empty space
From Mars to Venus
Arriving at an earthly realm
As foretold by ancient stars

This alien
Body blends
Inconspicuously

Why do earthlings believe
Their eyes
Glance
The hair
The breasts
Decide
All is in place
Deem biology irrelevant
Call me 'she'
While rebelling
Against invasion

This alien
Body blends
It is beautiful

Why did I
Dream this possibility
Hop on a ship
Leave the furious
Red planet
Settle on Earth

Earthlings need
Celestial wonders

A World Where Transness Thrives

a human experience
foreign
to the language
so does not exist
an enigmatic state
defying
common sense

worldviews once
hardened
are vigorously defended
against
invading ideas
he can never be she
nor she can ever be he

transness thrives in
spirit
a wild world, vast
rebellious
where being is
mystery
an encounter with the
Sacred

Unruly Femininity

my femininity like
a chestnut mare
nostrils flared
stomping in a grassy field
skin twitching
tail swishing
to swipe distractions

my femininity like
a stage actor
refusing
to bow
the audience
claps and roars

they saw
a performance
I staged
a rebellion

Black Transfemme Enby

Transwomen
Are women
They aptly declare
Who speaks for me
As if I could ever
Brave the mirror
No matter how femme
I present myself
Or however many
Times I'm called
Miss or ma'am
And declare my
Black womanhood
When I have lived a distinct
Life as a wounded
Black male

I'm a rule-breaker
A gender rebel
Masculine feminine
Boy girl
Churned chocolate
Vanilla swirl
A color-blocked
Human whole
Sharing earth
With other beings

Woman-Owned

I slink into a sex shop
That's woman-owned
An October day
In Provincetown
I tip-toe around
Avoiding all eyes
Scanning the objects
As I pick out one
For me
Or two
I think of bodies
Sensual pleasures
Their birthright to feel

Alone or together
With whoever they choose
However many they choose
Bodies not chased or
Controlled or shamed but
Shared and
Welcomed into
I pay for my items
And strut out

Temptation (An Invitation)

magic
pills sprout a bosom
defiant of fleshy frames
dainty peaks protrude daringly
searching soft hands
the moist lips of a
lover

part four

Trees

I envy the trees
They rudely shed
Leaves at your doorstep
Stand naked
Battered by wind
Frost
Rain
Yet rooted
Everything they need
Within

The seasons change
They bloom in defiance
Pollinating with plumes of ecstasy
Leaves return
Again
The summer heat
Drought
Lightning
Birds nest
Playing with branches
The trees withstand all
There is love in their stillness
Repeating year after year
Until my bones are bent and brittle
Yet the trees grow stronger
Thicker
Tougher
Their story held
Within

The Magic in the Moments

Easter Sunday
Kids roam the house
Faces gleaming
Searching for colorful plastic
Eggs left by a bunny
  An adorable
Fluffy
Creature without hands
Sneaking into houses
While all are sleeping
Leaving fun gifts and candy

Isn't there always something
Lurking in the night
Giving or taking
Sometimes both

Santa with his giant sleigh and flying reindeers
The tooth fairy gathering children's teeth
          and leaving cash
The world is just so giving
Magical
At some point
We stop believing in fairy tales
The world doesn't seem as giving

The magic was never
The being sneaking
In our homes at night
But the ordinary stuff
We truly can't explain
Hearing a song
Being moved to tears
Reading a story
Feeling joy
Holding a warm cup
Feeling peace
Laughing with a friend
Reliving that laughter again
Then you have felt the
Magic that lurks
In the moments

Seeing You Seeing Me

when you are you
and I am me
you help me be
in you I see
beauty

when you can be you
and I can be me
we can be messy
and silly and needy
we bring our
authenticity

when I accept you
and you accept me
we live
courageously
it's not easy
we're different
you see
the world gave us
this moment
to be

ANTONNETTE ASARE is a Black nonbinary transfeminine poet and writer from the Bronx, New York. She writes from the nexus of multiple identities, seeking joy, meaning, and beauty in the mundane yet miraculous moments of everyday life. Her work courageously explores both the shadows and brightness of her experience as part of a journey toward authenticity, connection, and living in alignment with her values. She reminds readers of the preciousness of life and the importance of living it fully alongside all the beings who share this moment in time.

www.aasare.net • sp@aasare.net

www.ingramcontent.com/pod-product-compliance
Lightning Source LLC
Chambersburg PA
CBHW040201160726
48006CB00014B/1848